Sports IN ACTION

Gymnastics in Action

Bobbie Kalman & John Crossingham

Illustrations by Bonna Rouse

Photographs by Marc Crabtree

Crabtree Publishing Company

www.crabtreebooks.com

Created by Bobbie Kalman

Dedicated by Rebecca Sjonger
For Avery Elizabeth Malloch

Editor-in-Chief
Bobbie Kalman

Writing team
Bobbie Kalman
John Crossingham

Editorial director
Niki Walker

Project editor
Rebecca Sjonger

Editors
Amanda Bishop
Kathryn Smithyman

Art director
Robert MacGregor

Design
Margaret Amy Salter
Campbell Creative
  Services (cover)

Production coordinator
Heather Fitzpatrick

Photo research
Rebecca Sjonger
Jaimie Nathan

Special thanks to
Candace Dickson, Kelsey Dickson, Jennifer Giancaterino, Melissa Giancaterino, Sabrina Giancaterino, Shawn Pellizari, Jenna Stamp, Nicole Taylor, Mary Jane Grantham, Jason Lang, Gymnastics Energy Training Centre

Consultant
Luan Peszek, Director of Publications
USA Gymnastics

Photographs
Marc Crabtree: front cover, back cover, title page, 5, 8, 12, 13, 14, 15, 16, 17, 19, 20, 21, 22, 23, 24, 25, 26, 27, 28, 29
Other images by Digital Stock and PhotoDisc

Illustrations
All illustrations by Bonna Rouse except the following:
Trevor Morgan: page 9 (bottom left)
Margaret Amy Salter: chapter heading

Crabtree Publishing Company

www.crabtreebooks.com   1-800-387-7650
Copyright © **2003 CRABTREE PUBLISHING COMPANY.**
All rights reserved. No part of this publication may be reproduced, stored in a retrieval system or be transmitted in any form or by any means, electronic, mechanical, photocopying, recording, or otherwise, without the prior written permission of Crabtree Publishing Company. In Canada: We acknowledge the financial support of the Government of Canada through the Canada Book Fund for our publishing activities.

Printed in the USA/092017/HF20170725

Library of Congress Cataloging-in-Publication Data
Kalman, Bobbie
  Gymnastics in action / Bobbie Kalman & John Crossingham; illustrations by Bonna Rouse; photographs by Marc Crabtree.
    p. cm. — (Sports in action)
Includes index.
This book introduces basic gymnastics skills, styles of gymnastics, equipment, and competitions in the sport of gymnastics.
ISBN 0-7787-0330-4 (RLB) — ISBN 0-7787-0350-9 (pbk.)
  1. Gymnastics—Juvenile literature. [1. Gymnastics.] I. Crossingham, John. II. Rouse, Bonna, ill. III. Crabtree, Marc, ill. IV. Title. V. Series.
  GV461.3 .K35 2003
  796.44—dc21
                                                    LC 2002014303

Published in Canada
Crabtree Publishing
616 Welland Ave.
St. Catharines, Ontario
L2M 5V6

Published in the United States
Crabtree Publishing
PMB 59051
350 Fifth Avenue, 59th Floor
New York, New York 10118

Published in the United Kingdom
Crabtree Publishing
Maritime House
Basin Road North, Hove
BN41 1WR

Published in Australia
Crabtree Publishing
3 Charles Street
Coburg North
VIC, 3058

Contents

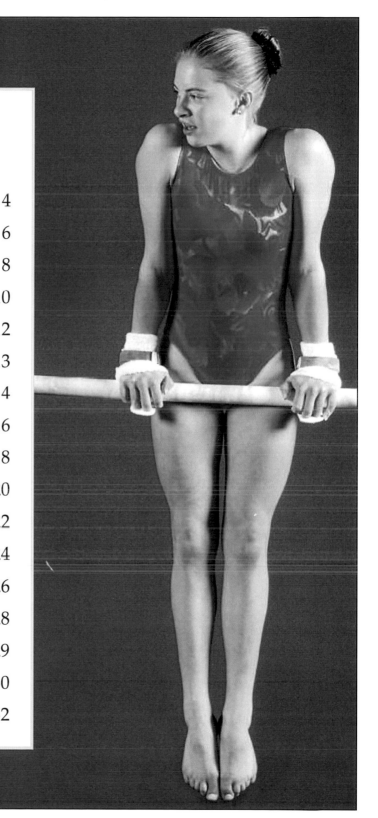

What is gymnastics?

Gymnastics is a sport that tests a person's **flexibility**, balance, and strength. This sport also requires speed, **agility**, and courage. People who perform gymnastics are called **gymnasts**. A series of gymnastics moves is called a **routine**. Skilled gymnasts perform tough routines and make them look easy.

Gymnastics is divided into different **events**. The events are based on skills gymnasts perform on equipment. Many boys and girls use gymnastics to challenge themselves and have fun. You are never too young to start learning gymnastics. In fact, many gymnasts begin training by the time they can walk.

*Boys' gymnastics events include **pommel horse**, **rings**, **parallel bars**, **horizontal bar**, **floor exercise**, and **vault**. Girls' events include vault, **uneven bars**, **balance beam**, and floor exercise.*

What's your game?

There are two main styles of gymnastics—**artistic** and **rhythmic**. Rhythmic gymnastics is done on a floor mat and uses **hand apparatus** such as clubs, a rope, a hoop, a ball, or a ribbon. The other gymnastics events are artistic. This book features the basics of the sport and mainly covers artistic gymnastics. Rhythmic gymnastics is discussed at the end.

Competitions

Both gymnastics styles have competitions. The gymnasts' routines are scored by judges. The judges give scores based on a routine's difficulty and how well the gymnast performs the skills it includes. Gymnastics competitions are exciting, but there's more to the sport than winning ribbons and trophies. You can have a lot of fun before you even think of competing!

Building blocks

It takes years of practice to become a skilled gymnast. **Progressions** help gymnasts advance. Gymnasts make progressions when they perfect basic moves and then develop them into more difficult moves. For example, the gymnast on the left perfected the **splits** on the floor before trying the move on the rings. To progress, gymnasts must be patient and fit.

*Girls and boys both use the **vault table**, which is a new piece of gymnastics equipment.*

Gymnasts spend many hours training. Practicing a lot helps them perfect their form.

Welcome to the gym

Gymnasts practice and perform their skills in buildings called **gymnasiums**, or gyms for short. Gyms come in all shapes and sizes. Most are quite large and have very high ceilings. Some gyms also have seating for spectators.

uneven bars

balance beam

floor

Bouncing floor

In gymnastics, even the "**floor**" is a piece of equipment. The floor is a platform that sits on the real gym floor and is covered by a mat. It is 39 feet (12 m) by 39 feet (12 m). The surface is made of wood or synthetic materials. It has a layer of small springs that helps gymnasts perform spins, leaps, and tumbling moves by absorbing the impact of their landings.

Some gyms have **pits**, which are big holes in the floor that are lined with foam and filled with foam blocks. Gymnasts land in pits when they practice **dismounts**, or getting off the equipment. Thick floor mats are also used to protect gymnasts as they practice their moves. Sometimes these mats are placed below floor level, like a pit. Gymnasts feel more confident knowing that a pit or mat will cushion their landings.

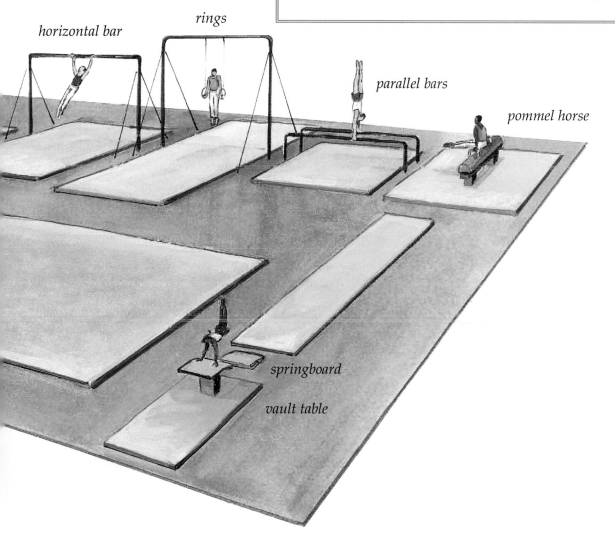

horizontal bar

rings

parallel bars

pommel horse

springboard

vault table

The essentials

Gymnasts wear sleek, stretchy clothing that allows them to move freely. The most common item is a one-piece suit called a **leotard**, although many gymnasts now wear two-piece outfits such as the one on the left. Gymnasts may also practice in a comfortable pair of shorts and a T-shirt. Before and after practicing, they wear tracksuits or sweatpants to keep their muscles warm. Besides clothing, there are a few other items that are important. You can carry all your gear in a gym bag.

If you have long hair, tie it back so that it doesn't get in your way. You may also be required to take off your jewelry before you enter the gym. Never chew gum while doing gymnastics—you could choke on it!

When your hands grip and rub against the bars or rings, they may get blisters. You can wear hand covers called **grips** for protection. To keep your hands from slipping on the bars, rub a light layer of **chalk** powder on them.

chalk

boy's hand grip

girl's hand grip

Gymnastics may make you sweat, so keep a towel handy for drying yourself off. You should always have a bottle of water nearby, so you can replace the fluids you lose when you sweat.

Rhythmic gymnastics has its own gear. These items include ribbons, balls, hoops, ropes, and clubs (see page 31). These colorful pieces add to the beauty of the event. Rhythmic gymnasts also wear **half-shoes**. A half-shoe covers only the toe and ball of the foot.

Warming up

You must always stretch before any practice or competition. Doing so helps maintain your flexibility. Some of these warm-up moves can be difficult at first. Perform the stretches slowly, and your flexibility will eventually improve. Activities such as skipping rope and running are also good ways to warm up.

Toe touches

Sit on the floor with your legs in front of you. Reach past your toes with your hands. Try to touch your nose to your knees.

neck stretch

Tilt your head forward. Keep your chin down and slowly roll your head toward one shoulder and then the other. Do not roll your head backward. Repeat five times.

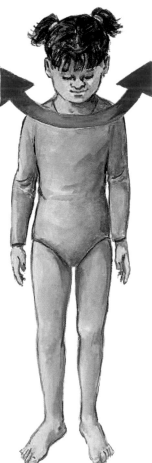

Arm circles

Swing your arms in large circles. Make the motions smaller and smaller until your arms are moving in tiny circles straight out to the sides. Reverse the direction, starting with small movements and ending with large circles.

Split stretches

These stretches can be done from a splits position. Don't worry if you cannot do the splits yet—just try to sit with your legs straight and as far apart as possible. Repeat each stretch five to ten times.

Bring your chest toward your thigh and reach for your toes. Switch sides.

Reach out in front of you and try to touch your chest flat to the floor. Keep your back straight.

Reach your left hand over your head toward your right foot. Switch hands and reach for your left foot.

Up and over

Sit with your legs straight and your hands at your sides. Lie back onto your shoulders. Bring your legs up and over your head until your toes touch the ground. Slowly return to the sitting position. Keep your legs straight. Repeat five times.

Bridge

Lie on your back and bend your knees. Place your feet on the floor with the heels close to your hips. Put your hands on the floor beside your head with your fingers pointing at your feet. Arch your back as you push your hips into the air. Straighten your legs.

Coaches

You should never do gymnastics by yourself. Always have a **coach** watching you. A coach helps you correct mistakes before they become bad habits. He or she can offer you advice on good exercises to perform and the right foods to eat. Most importantly, a coach is there to keep you safe as you learn.

Spotting the moves

To boost your confidence, your coach may also act as a **spotter**. A spotter supports and guides your body as you try new moves.

Keep it safe

Many gymnastics events are performed above the ground or involve high-speed jumps and leaps. No matter how confident you feel or how eager you are to try new moves, you should never work on gymnastics equipment without your coach present. Remember the importance of progressions and moving gradually from basic to more advanced moves. Focus on learning and practicing each move properly as you develop and perfect your skills. Doing so will make the time you spend practicing gymnastics much safer.

Positions please!

Gymnastics has its own language. It may sound like regular English, but when coaches ask for a **pike**, they don't want a fish! A pike is a body position. Every move and position has its own name. There are four main body positions, and they are among the first things to learn. Gymnasts use these positions in all events. They end every routine with a **layout**, shown bottom right.

The tuck: Crouch down with your knees against your chest and wrap you hands around your knees.

The pike: Bend at the hips and keep your legs straight. Touch your hands to the floor or the back of your ankles.

The layout: Raise your arms and form a straight line from your toes to the tips of your fingers.

The straddle: Spread your legs and raise your arms out to the sides. Keep your back straight and your face forward.

Basic moves

Once you have a coach and a proper place to practice, you can begin to learn some basic moves. Although there are hundreds of gymnastics moves, the four shown here are great for starting. They will develop your flexibility and balance. Whether you are working on the floor, the balance beam, or the rings, you will always come back to these moves.

Handstand

The most important part of doing a handstand is keeping your back, legs, and arms straight. Your knees bend only as your feet prepare to leave the ground.

1. Stretch your arms straight up. Step forward with one leg. Bend this leg and lower your chest toward your front thigh with your hands moving toward the floor. Your other leg remains straight and will begin to lift as you bend forward.

2. Place your hands on the floor. Your arms, back, and raised leg should be in a straight line. Lift your other leg off the ground.

3. Swing your body up into a straight position. Raise your first leg straight up and move your second leg alongside it. Your leg movements will be like scissors closing. Your whole body should be in a straight line.

Forward roll

This move is like a tumbling somersault. Practice forward rolls on a soft mat.

Bend at the knees and waist. Stretch your arms in front of you. Tuck your chin to your chest and push off with your legs. Land on your palms and roll forward, bringing your legs over your body. Put your feet on the floor, stand up, and return to your original position.

Backward roll

This move is similar to the forward roll, but you roll backward.

1. Take the same starting position as in the forward roll. Fall back onto your bottom. Bend your elbows and place your hands behind your head near your ears.

2. Keeping your knees bent, swing your legs backward over your body. Balance on your palms and shoulders.

3. As your legs begin to fall back to the ground, push off with your hands. Place your feet on the ground and rise up into a crouch.

Cartwheel

Cartwheels are important because they lead to many other similar skills, such as **round-offs** and **side aerials**. These instructions are for a left cartwheel

1. Stand facing in the direction you wish to move. Raise your arms above your head and lift your left leg. Your weight is on your right leg.

2. As you set your left foot down in front of you, kick up your right leg and tip yourself onto your hands. Your hands should be about shoulder-width apart, and your legs should be straight and in the splits throughout the move.

3. Swing your legs over you and allow your weight to shift to your right side. Place your right foot on the ground and put your weight on it. Keep moving your left leg until your left foot is on the ground next to your right foot and you are standing upright.

Do not bend forward or backward at the hips during the cartwheel.

The **arabesque** is a common pose. Gymnasts balance on one leg and hold their other leg straight out behind them. Their heads are held up and their backs are arched.

Tumbling runs are very quick and can include several **elements**, or moves. The moves are connected without any pauses.

Floor exercise

Floor routines are performed by both boys and girls. A routine lasts around a minute. The floor is the best place for you to start because you do not have to worry about falling as much as you do in other events.

Routines

Floor routines consist of **tumbling runs**. In a tumbling run, a gymnast performs a series of moves from one corner of the floor to the other. These runs are made up of moves such as round-offs, front **handsprings**, and **saltos**, or flips. Gymnasts can change direction with **transition moves** such as rolls.

Different styles

Girls and boys do not perform the same floor routines. Girls perform their routines to music, and they focus on dance as well as tumbling. Boys perform routines that are based on strength, balance, and tumbling. Boys may also do moves that are usually seen on the pommel horse (see page 22). In the corners, boys hold balances and arabesques for a few seconds. Girls pose and dance in and out of each corner.

Building speed

In a floor routine, a gymnast performs a few quick steps, called a **run-up**, to gain speed for tumbling moves such as round-offs, handsprings, and tucks. The gymnast moves at a fast pace and does a **hurdle** to connect the run with the first tumbling move. The hurdle is a transition move in which a gymnast bounds off one foot and brings both feet down to spring into the tumbling move.

The run-up is also used in the vault event. Gymnasts run up and jump onto the springboard (see page 20).

Staying limber

To do a **front limber**, begin by going into a handstand. Don't stop moving your legs once they are straight up. Keep moving them until your feet are on the floor behind your head. Raise your upper body to stand up. A **back limber** is similar to a front limber, but you arch backward into a handstand. Keep moving your legs until your feet hit the floor and you can stand upright again. The limber will prepare you to progress to a **walkover**.

To complete a front limber, lift your upper body until you are standing up straight.

Balancing act

Only girls compete on the balance beam. The beam is four feet (1.2 m) off the ground and sixteen feet long (4.9 m), but it is only four inches (10 cm) wide! Gymnasts not only step along the beam, but they also perform many moves on it. They may do poses, handstands, walkovers, and even saltos!

One step at a time

On the beam, the key is to look straight ahead—not down. To get used to walking this way, young gymnasts begin by practicing along a four-inch (10 cm) wide strip on the floor. As they improve, they progress to working on a beam that is lower than normal. Eventually, they become skilled enough to practice on beams that are raised to the regular height.

Follow the routine

A typical beam routine lasts about a minute and a half. It begins when the gymnast gets on the beam with a move called a **mount**. The mount can be anything from a simple leap to a salto in the air. On the beam, gymnasts can perform a variety of moves, including **split leaps**, **back tucks**, handstands, and walkovers. They also do dance moves and poses. The routine has to flow smoothly from move to move.

Dismount

The final move is the dismount, or getting off the beam. Most gymnasts finish with an exciting dismount because it is the last move that the judges see. Beginners use basic body positions, such as the tuck or straddle, as part of their dismounts. As they become comfortable on the beam, gymnasts work on more impressive dismounts. They practice moves such as round-offs and eventually work toward performing aerial dismounts.

*Gymnasts usually practice moves such as this **stag** on the floor before trying them on the beam.*

As a dismount, try one of the positions described on page 13. This girl is in the pike position.

Vault

In the past, the vault event involved boys and girls leaping over a tall **vaulting horse**. Girls went over the width of the horse, whereas boys went over its length. In 2001, however, the International Gymnastics Federation introduced a new piece of equipment called a vault table, which is replacing the horse. A major change to the event has resulted—boys and girls go over the table the same way. There will be a changeover period before tables are found in all gyms.

New equipment, old moves

The basics of the event are the same, no matter which vault gymnasts use. Gymnasts run toward the horse or table and then jump onto a springboard, which pops them up into the air. They push off the table or horse with their hands. In the air, gymnasts can perform flips or spins. They land on a soft mat on the other side of the vault. Gymnasts must **stick** their landings, which means they have to land on both feet at the same time, with no wobbles or extra steps.

The run-up rundown

Before trying the vault, beginners use a springboard and a mat to practice their run-ups. Use this drill to develop a smooth run-up:

- run on the balls of your feet and go faster as you near the springboard
- just before the board, do a hurdle
- bring your feet together and land on the end of the board
- in the air, reach up with your arms
- bend at the knees to soften your landing and land on the mat with both feet
- be sure to stick the landing

Practice different body positions in midair, such as a tuck or a layout, which is shown above.

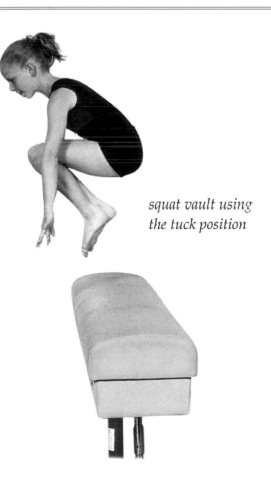

squat vault using the tuck position

Putting it together

Once you have a good run-up, you can add the vault to your practice. Try the **squat vault**, shown left, or a handspring as one of your first moves. Both are simple and allow you to stay upright. You can really focus on the different steps in vaulting. No matter which move you perform, remember to watch the vault—not the springboard— during your run-up.

The vaulting horse (left) is now being replaced by the vault table (opposite page).

21

Pommel horse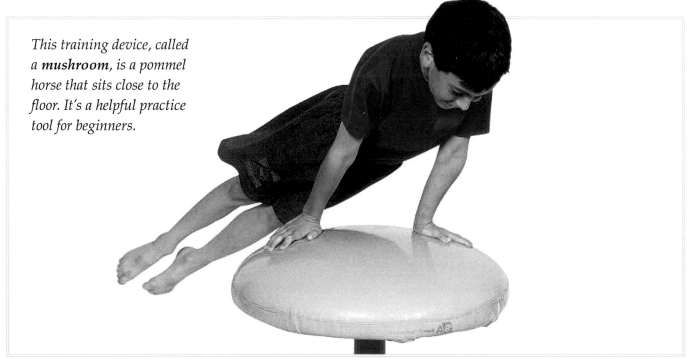

The pommel horse is an event in which only boys compete. It requires upper-body strength and quick hands. The horse looks like a vaulting horse, but it has two handles, called **pommels**, on top. Gymnasts don't run and leap over the pommel horse, as they do over the vault. Instead, they perform leg moves while balancing on it with their hands. No other part of their bodies can touch the horse. Rather than mounting the pommel horse using a springboard, you use your arms to lift yourself onto it. Once you are on the horse, try not to let your legs, feet, or bottom touch it. You must start with simple exercises at first. Practice shifting your weight from one arm to the other, and try to keep your body straight above the horse. Performing basic moves builds up your arm strength and balance, which are the keys to performing well on the pommel horse. This event came from the sport of bull riding over 2,500 years ago. Competitors held on to the horns of jumping, kicking bulls and tried to ride them.

*This training device, called a **mushroom**, is a pommel horse that sits close to the floor. It's a helpful practice tool for beginners.*

Hands up

An easy move to start with is the **stoop through**. To do this move, lift both legs between your arms and bring your backside above the horse. Most pommel horse moves are more difficult than the stoop through. **Scissors**, **swings**, and **leg circles** all have one thing in common—you have to lift up your arms one at a time so that your legs can pass underneath them. You have to be strong enough to switch your weight from one arm to the other during the move.

Now try more

To complete a 30-second routine, gymnasts need great **endurance**, or strength to keep going without tiring. Building a routine takes patience and planning. At first, gymnasts learn how to perform pommel horse moves one at a time. As their skills improve, they are able to string the moves together to form a routine.

(above) ***Single-leg swings*** *use a straddle position over the horse.*

Raise the bar

Bar events have some of the most exciting moves in gymnastics. Doing chin-ups is a good way to strengthen your arms for these moves. On the uneven bars, female gymnasts spin, twist, and swing between two sets of bars. The height of the two bars varies depending on the height of the gymnast. The bars are set high enough for the gymnast to swing on them without hitting the floor. A routine lasts about 30 seconds and ends with a dismount.

A bar routine should flow from one move to the next without pauses or extra swings.

Boys' bars

The horizontal bar, or **high bar**, is a boys' event. Unlike the uneven bars, this event has only one bar, which is over eight feet (2.4 m) off the ground. When learning on the high bar, most young gymnasts lower the bar to about five feet (1.5 m). Routines last from fifteen to 30 seconds and include swings, **release moves**, and dismounts. For release moves a gymnast must let go of and then regrasp the bar.

Gripping news

There are four bar grips. In a routine, gymnasts frequently switch their grips. The overgrip is used most often, and it is the one that beginners learn first. As you progress, you may also use one of the other grips shown below.

overgrip

undergrip

mixed grip

eagle grip

Out for a swing

Before performing any of the more difficult bar moves, you must first learn to swing. When swinging back and forth, it is best to use an overgrip. Get moving by thrusting your legs and hips forward as though you are on a swing set. Once you start swinging, try to keep your body straight. Hold the bar tightly as you swing forward. Bend at the wrists. As you swing backward, loosen your grasp and let your hands slide back around the bar. As you swing forward again, readjust your grasp. Don't forget to chalk your hands or wear grips.

The horizontal bar offers boys plenty of swinging room. Beginners spend a lot of time practicing swinging to get used to the feeling of the motion.

Mount, spin, dismount!

A basic routine on the uneven or horizontal bars consists of a mount, a series of moves, and a dismount. The pace of a routine blends fast and slow moves, but the gymnast cannot stop or pause between them. The routine must flow smoothly.

For a front-support mount, grab the bar with an overgrip and then jump and lift yourself up. The top of your thighs should touch the bar, and your arms should be straight. This mount is often performed with the move seen below.

Starting low

It's a good idea to start learning moves on a low bar. You can move to a higher bar as your confidence and skills grow. The **front-support mount** is a good way to get started. This move involves simply pulling yourself up onto the bar, as shown top left.

In circles

Another basic move on the bars is the **circle**. Like most moves, circles come in many styles. Starting from a front-support mount, an easy move is the **back-hip circle**, shown left. As your body comes around the bar, you end up right where you began—in a front-support position.

Grips change with your direction. Your thumbs should point in the direction in which you are spinning.

So many moves!

Bar moves challenge the strength of gymnasts. In **stride circles**, gymnasts spin around with one leg on either side of the bar. They perform **sole circles** (left) with their hands and the soles of their feet on the same bar! In a **basket**, gymnasts use a type of pike position—they stick their legs up between the bar and their chests. Gymnasts change their grips to suit each move. For some release moves they let go of the bar entirely and regrasp it with a different grip.

A perfect landing

At first, dismounts are mainly about landing safely on both feet. For more advanced gymnasts, the dismount is often one of the most complex moves in their routines. They often use moves they learned for floor routines, especially front and back flips. Before gymnasts leave the bar, they perform several swings or circles to build up speed. They then fly off the bar into flips or spins before landing on both feet. As the gymnasts let go, they watch the ground. They bend their knees slightly to absorb the impact of the landing.

*The **flyaway** is a very difficult but beautiful dismount. Some gymnasts perform multiple flips and twists during a flyaway dismount.*

Parallel bars

The parallel bars event is for boys. The two long bars are set up so that they are a little more than shoulder-width apart. Parallel bars require a great deal of timing, balance, and coordination.

Hold that for a moment

Most of the skills on parallel bars involve swinging and moves such as saltos. Beginners often use a lot of **holds**, but they use them less as they progress. One hold move is the **L-support hold**, shown below. Gymnasts form an "L" with their legs and upper bodies.

Lift me up

Gymnasts must be able to lift themselves with their arms in order to perform on the parallel bars. To build up strength, practice lifting up your body between the bars. Start with one hand on each bar and have your elbows bent. Straighten your arms slowly to lift up your body. Hold your position and then gradually lower yourself. Progress to a handstand and other more difficult moves as your upper-body strength increases.

(left) A handstand can be done on the bars. Gymnasts sometimes balance on one hand.

The L-support hold requires strong arm, chest, stomach, and leg muscles.

Rings

The rings event is for boys. It has a lot in common with the parallel bars—both events test strength and involve hold moves. The rings event requires more upper-body strength than the parallel bars or any other event. The rings usually hang eight feet (2.4 m) off the ground. Young gymnasts practice on rings that hang lower, however. Once they have mastered the basic skills, they can have the rings raised. The rings hang freely. They are not fixed in place like the parallel bars. A gymnast must keep the rings as still as possible while performing his routine. Beginners start by hanging on the rings and counting to ten. They then progress to practicing various hold moves. Next, they try swings and eventually work up to more advanced moves.

Lower the rings so that your coach can hold them still. Now you can practice without the rings moving. As you improve, your coach will not have to hold the rings.

Rhythmic gymnastics

Rhythmic gymnastics is performed on the floor by girls. This style of gymnastics has grown in popularity since it began as a training exercise in the 1950s. In 1996, it was performed at the Olympics for the first time. Rhythmic gymnastics doesn't have the tumbling runs or acrobatic flips of the floor exercise. Instead, gymnasts perform rolls, leaps, and turns while working with one of the apparatus shown on the opposite page.

Each apparatus has its own event. No matter which apparatus a gymnast uses, she must be in constant balanced motion with it. The apparatus almost becomes part of her body. For example, in the **ball event**, a gymnast tosses the ball in the air as she drops down into the splits. She then catches the ball and lets it roll along one arm, behind her head, and along the other arm into her other hand. A rhythmic gymnast must be especially flexible and graceful.

Tools of the trade

There are five types of apparatus a rhythmic gymnast can use—clubs, a rope, a ball, a hoop, or a ribbon. She performs her routine to her choice of music. A routine lasts about a minute and a half. Competitions also include a group event, in which team members perform a routine together.

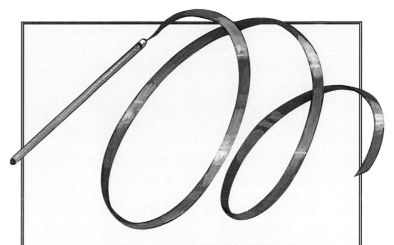

A gymnast twirls and streaks the ribbon through the air, creating beautiful patterns. She can also toss and catch it by the handle.

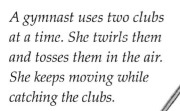

A gymnast uses two clubs at a time. She twirls them and tosses them in the air. She keeps moving while catching the clubs.

A gymnast tosses and bounces the ball. She also rolls it over her body. She holds the ball as little as possible as she turns and rolls with it.

A gymnast jumps with the rope, winds it around her body, and tosses and catches it with one or two hands.

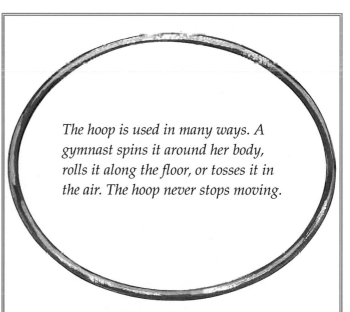

The hoop is used in many ways. A gymnast spins it around her body, rolls it along the floor, or tosses it in the air. The hoop never stops moving.

31

Glossary

Note: Boldfaced words that are defined in the book may not appear in the glossary.

agility The ability to move quickly and easily

back tuck A backward flip in the air, with the legs tucked against the chest

dismount A move used to get off equipment

event A gymnastics activity involving a certain piece of equipment or style of movement

flexibility The ability to bend the body easily into various positions

handspring A flip that moves the gymnast quickly from an upright position to balancing on the hands and then back to an upright position

hold A still position on the parallel bars or rings, used to show strength

leg circle A move on the pommel horse that involves the legs and body quickly circling the horse

mount A move used to get onto equipment

round-off A cartwheel with the legs held together during the landing

routine A series of smoothly connected gymnastics moves

salto A flip or somersault in the air

scissors A pommel horse move made by swinging straightened legs back and forth from the hips

side aerial A flip in the air, which the gymnast performs to the side, rather than forward or backward

split leap A jump with the legs spread straight out to either side or in front and back of the body

splits A position in which the legs are spread straight out to either side or in front and back of the body

springboard A board with springs that is used to propel the gymnast upward

swing A move on the pommel horse that requires the hips and legs to swing upward

transition move A short quick action that links two more complicated moves

walkover A move that requires a gymnast to go from an upright position to a balanced position on the hands, and then to drop one leg and then the other to touch the ground before straightening up

Index